A Wife's Guide to

Inspiring a Great Dad

D.J.Young

www.Wisdom4Dads.com

Duane J. Young
Wisdom4Dads

djyoung@wisdom4dads.com
www.wisdom4dads.com

A Wife's Guide
To Inspiring a Great Dad

D. J. Young
(c) 2009

All Rights Reserved

ISBN: 1451592728
EAN: 9781451592726

All definitions are taken from online Merriam-Webster Dictionary.

All Scriptures are taken from the Authorized King James Version.

Dedication

I dedicate this book to my wife, Kathy, my daughter, Melissa, and my daughters-in-law, Mel and Vickie. Each one believes in her man to be a dad in their home. They understand that to love and support their husband in his role, as dad, does not detract from their significance as a wife and mother. God bless you!

D. J. Young

Titles By D.J. Young

Eight Wonders Of Being A Father

Eight Spiritual Wonders Of Being A Father

Adult Children and Their Dads
  —*The Eight Needs Of Dads*

You're Still Their Dad
  —*Fathering Your Adult Children*

The Tests Of Youth
  —*Guiding Children To Maturity*

Dad, Father, Grandfather
  —*The Three Phases Of Fatherhood*

Seven Pillars Of A Father's House
  —*Training and Discipline of Children*

Twelve Training Gifts
  —*How Fathers Train Children*

Table of Contents

CHAPTER ONE
Encouragement:
Wind in His Sail 1

CHAPTER TWO
Affirmation:
Helm and Rudder 7

CHAPTER THREE
Course Correction:
Finding True North 13

CHAPTER FOUR
Leadership:
Who is Captain of What Boat? 19

CHAPTER FIVE
Correction, Discipline, and Training:
Charting the Course 25

CHAPTER SIX
God's Idea of a Dad:
He Clothes His Children 31

CHAPTER SEVEN
A Dad's Ministry:
Giving Life 37

CHAPTER EIGHT
Improving Communication Skills:
When to Paint the Boat 43

Preface

s a wife you *can* inspire your husband to become a great dad. As DJ's wife, I can verify that he has helped me to become a mother of great worth.

As mothers we feel we can always do more, be better, or improve ourselves. My role, as mother, is important and significant, but I struggle anyway. We chose to make it our priority for me to stay at home with the children when they were little, but I struggle anyway. I love my children and am willing to sacrifice a great deal for each of them, but I struggle anyway.

And so, in my questioning I have to turn to the Lord:

- Am I doing enough?
- Do I have to, or need to, or want to make this decision now?
- How can I possibly not overprotect, when we live in a world where protection is so necessary?
- Have I thought far enough ahead for the potential consequences of my actions on each child's life?
- How can I possibly be sure of each child's health—emotional, physical, spiritual, psychological, and financial?

I'm convinced the difference between a good and great dad is his wife. Just as the difference between DJ being a good or great dad depends on me!

My husband is good as a dad because of his willingness to sacrifice. His sacrifice is demonstrated as he loves our children, and toward me when he notices I need a "break". He is selfless when it comes to our family. But I believe he became a Great Dad for *my* sake, not necessarily the kids' sake. In other words, he loves our children but he loves me more! This, too, I struggle with because it sounds so selfish on my part—but it's true.

When our children were in our home, he often took up the slack in discipline, in getting me out of the house, out of town to see friends, and in thinking of my needs even before I did. Even now when our grandchildren are in our home, he is quick to see the need I have for help and for relating to each precious life with care and grace.

He steps in beyond what I do presently in each of our adult children's lives. As a great dad he supports their role as parents. He is quick to reach out with a phone call, a money gift or a note of acknowledgment of the love we have for them and their family.

To summarize, I love being a mother and grandmother, but I am a healthy, vibrant mother and grandmother because my husband became a great dad.

—Kathy Young

Introduction

ince this is "a wife's guide," I will address you personally. No one plays a more vital role in shaping a man toward becoming a great dad than you, his wife. Your husband may not be aware of the importance of your influence, or how much you impact his willingness and ability to become a great parent.

Let's think of parenting as a sea with seasons, storms, deep waters, shallow waters, and swift and gentle meandering currents. In an actual boating excursion, most men would run headlong into the adventure, but as a parent many dads move ahead slowly, and only after much encouragement.

In various other areas of life—work, sports, or hobbies— dads are much more confident. They have been actively engaged in these activities for a long time and derive much joy from them. But parenting is new territory and therefore a bit frightening, especially since a new parent just sees the tip of the iceberg. The unknown is what makes it most terrifying.

When a man first learns that he will be a father, he already begins to suspect his inadequacies. TV shows have had the public laughing hysterically over a new dad's ineptness. He doesn't understand morning sickness, food cravings, mood swings, or tears of joy. He may feel trapped in a woman's world.

After the birth of his first child, he is suddenly cast into the world of parenthood—as a matter of fact, he is now a dad. He finds himself in unfamiliar territory. Since he hasn't read any reliable books about it, hasn't seriously discussed what to expect with more experienced fathers, or taken any classes on how to be a dad, you are his most reliable resource.

It is not easy for him to take advice from you on how to be a good dad. When he asks his buddies, they react with their usual macho humor, while you find it difficult to penetrate his wall of insecurity and fear of the unknown. But if you don't help him, he is more likely to become discouraged. If you are willing to guide him, he will have to be humble and teachable—qualities that you want to encourage.

You are not his mother, yet you need to assume a teaching role toward him. This task is separate from your role as his wife and your role as mother to your child. If you and your husband are willing to work together, you can be a wonderful influence and make a remarkable difference in your man. You will see him become a better man and a great dad.

It is important for you and your husband to understand that parenting is a long-term commitment. You will need each other's help. You influence each other's parenting style often complementing his rough edges. Remember, you can make or break the emerging dad. Most likely your husband does not rob you of your drive, enthusiasm and willingness to learn to parent. But you can easily diminish his drive and enthusiasm simply with a word, a look, a sigh, or apparent irritation at his clumsiness. Any of these gestures or attitudes can determine your husband's degree of involvement and willingness to grow in his role. You are his mate, lover and best friend, yet you can deprive him of his effectiveness as a dad without realizing it.

This book is titled A Wife's Guide to Inspiring a Great Dad because you and your husband are the two adults within the confines of the home who create the atmosphere in which your child flourishes. You need to nurture and support one another. Your children learn from your example, and in time the entire family will know how to encourage each other.

In the beginning your husband may appear as the weaker parent — less knowledgeable, less confident and less willing to ask for direction. You are in a strategic place to recognize the needs of your family and children, which are best met by both parents. Therefore you need to communicate those needs to your husband and encourage him to be involved every day in the life of his child. He needs your encouragement to step out and take a risk.

You and your husband will continue to grow in your parenting ability as you apply yourselves to become parents who know how to meet the needs of their children as babies, teens, young adults, and adult children. Your lives are interconnected with the lives of your children. The learning process takes place when your husband is willing to listen, and you are willing to encourage him in becoming a great dad. It is when you believe in him that he can continue to develop into a loving, caring dad. Therein lies your ministry. Blessed indeed is that man, husband and dad who calls you his own!

CHAPTER ONE

Encouragement:
Wind in His Sail

*Webster defines **encourage** as to "inspire with courage, spirit or hope, to spur on." Encourage is a transitive verb requiring an action directed toward another person or object, i.e., an unequivocal attempt to encourage <u>someone</u> with words, gestures, looks or emotional support.*

o encourage your husband in his parenting role is like putting wind in the sail of his boat as he ventures out onto the sea of parenthood. A sailboat in the water is not much fun if there is no wind. The absence of a breeze keeps the boat at the dock, moored with ropes. Regarding your husband's willingness to parent he can be bound with ropes of fear, or even terror.

As an astute wife, you recognize the powerful influence you have on your husband's willingness to leave the dock. If you are overbearing and critical your husband may retreat, doing less parenting and leaving more and more to you. Your relationship with him, and his relationship with your child, hangs in the balance here—an extremely delicate balance. You love each other and want to be each other's best friend. It is hard to imagine how much having a child changes your marriage.

Your husband no longer has your exclusive attention; the new baby does. Some days you may be too tired to give the usual attention and affection to your husband. You both experience deficiencies in areas where you were once very strong and affirming in your relationship. It becomes easier for him to focus more on his work, his sports and his hobbies, because there he feels confident. There he experiences peace instead of discomfort, contentment instead of doubt, and pleasure instead of pressure.

The comfortable life he had with you has suddenly vanished. He doesn't object all that much. After all, your newborn child has filled a big space in your hearts and lives. Suddenly he realizes more acutely his responsibility to provide for his growing family and begins to think about long-term needs, such as braces, college, weddings, and much more, all of which will require money. Work becomes vitally important to him.

There are moments when he misses time alone, the freedom to come and go at a moment's notice, the spur-of-the-moment weekend getaways and sleeping in late on Saturday morning. Still, he knows this is the better life; you are happy and he is happy, too.

A problem arises when you—his wife, best friend, and mother of his child—attempt to teach him—your husband, best friend, and father of your child—how to be a dad. He assumes that you possess more natural nurturing abilities as a mother and that it is easy for you to judge him concerning his lack of parenting skills. Popular TV shows have done their share over the past 30 years to portray men as clumsy and unfeeling dads: slow to learn, unable to assess what is going on, and failing to notice what is really important.

It is true that he cannot always see the whole picture when it comes to the children, therefore things can go wrong and backfire when he attempts to intervene in a situation. A sensible wife can diffuse much of this by learning to be an encourager, by inspiring her husband to try new approaches in his new role as dad. A good wife would never encourage her husband to do evil, be wicked, or bitter, or hold a grudge. She always encourages him to live a good and honest life, to trust in Jesus as his Lord and Savior, to pray and read God's Word and to address everyday problems that face his family.

You must be committed to encouraging your husband. Your husband is sensitive to your comments especially negative ones. By the same token, he thrives on your praise and encouragement. If you tell him, "Honey, the kids really love it when you read to them at bedtime," he will probably do more of it. If you scowl at him for taking too long with the stories or agitating the kids too much before they go to sleep, he is likely to retreat.

Often a wife recognizes her husband's ability in certain areas when he is not aware of his potential. If you pester him to "get with the program" or needle him with "when are you going to start . . ." he will be reluctant to follow through and will eventually be deprived of enjoying his area of expertise. It makes a world of difference how you boost or stifle him. Your approach directly impacts his motivation.

You run the household and care diligently for your child, but you may feel that your husband neither recognizes nor meets your needs—even if you had them printed on your forehead! Can you continue to encourage him under these circumstances?

Perhaps if his emotional cup were full, he could naturally reach out to you and meet some of your needs. To prevent an emotional drought, you and your husband must carve out time to nurture your relationship by focusing exclusively on each other, building each other up, refreshing one another with praise, laughter and relaxation. Reading books together on a regular basis is a good way to spend time with each other. It is important to have regular dates. A day of anticipation and an early bedtime for the baby can transform even a night at home into an event that rekindles your love and admiration.

Yes, encouragement is a great gift from you to your husband. In a similar manner, if you lack the wisdom and tact necessary to encourage your husband in his role as dad, you can deplete him in a short time and lose much in the aftermath.

Questions:

1 Give three examples of how your relationship with your husband changed after you had a child.

_____

_____

_____

_____

2 Give two examples of areas your husband needed to adjust his attitude before becoming a dad.

_____

_____

_____

_____

3 List three ways that you could encourage your husband in his new role as dad.

_____

_____

_____

_____

4 Give two examples of how being a Christian has impacted your ability to be an encourager.

_____

_____

_____

_____

5 Give three examples of how you and your husband continue to grow and mature as a couple while still being mom and dad to your children.

_____

_____

_____

_____

Prayer

*H*eavenly Father,
how often you encourage
me. You know what
helps me be a better
mom. Give me wisdom
and grace to help my
husband be a better dad.
Amen

CHAPTER TWO

Affirmation:
Helm and Rudder

he man who has a wise and loving wife is indeed a blessed man and is on his way to becoming a blessed dad. You can recognize gifts and talents in your husband that he may not be aware of. You can help him become a better dad through affirming him. You can help your husband today prepare for tomorrow. Affirmation entices him to enter the unknown path of fatherhood.

You can help him do more than he thinks he can; more than he wants to do and more than he has the time for. You consistently use positive words such as, "The kids love it when you..." or, "You are so good at..." You know that when you affirm your man, you and the children reap great benefits. Your children feel loved, cared for and nurtured by their dad, and you enjoy the peace that surrounds your everyday activities.

You have a variety of resources at your disposal. You can send affirming messages to your husband's heart any time you are not caught up in yourself or the demands of your role. As soon as you recognize the good your husband has done in relating to your children, you can affirm him with words like "You are so good at reading to the kids. They love it." He deserves a pat on the back from you for whatever he does with the children that is right and good.

If you are a jealous, insecure woman in your mother role, you are unlikely to welcome opportunities to affirm your husband when he is trying to be a good dad. If you let negative emotions control you, you may even put him down whenever the children show that they enjoy being with dad. Since you are around your children more, they may not demonstrate their appreciation to you in the same way they do toward their dad, whom they see only a fraction of the time.

Encouragement, like wind in his sail, has a destination in mind—a port of call if you will. Your husband wants to be a good dad. Once your children have left home he wants to have the peace of mind that flows from knowing he has done all he could to prepare them for life.

A boat is guided by the helm and rudder. Affirmation can be compared to the helm and rudder on dad's boat. It moves him in the right direction. This has nothing to do with manipulation or coercion. If you help him grow through loving affirmation, your husband will be grateful to you and follow your lead.

The dictionary tells us that to affirm means "to validate, to confirm". Confirmation is giving approval or new assurance of someone's validity. Where does your husband need validating? He may be very secure as husband, lover and friend. But as parent he may be on shaky ground. He wants validation in his role as dad and in his relationship with his children.

You are like the night watchman on the boat, looking out into the dark. You see land first. You see value in his role as dad long before he does. You can already see the fruit while he is inching into the uncharted territory of relating as a dad to your child. He needs and wants to know how he is doing.

You can validate his relationship building with each of his children. As he asks "Am I paying enough attention to Jimmy? Am I too hard on Julie?" you are his sounding board. Let him talk. What you say can make or break his willingness to invest time and energy. You also give him input about his conduct and attitudes. "You seem upset all the time. Why?" "You seem to treat Jimmy differently than Joe. Do you know why?" "When you do spend time with the kids, you just sit and play video games." When you give feedback to your husband with love and affection, the suggestions and even corrections you point out can develop him into the kind of dad he wants to be.

To validate and confirm effectively is an art, which you can learn if you are deeply interested in your husband's father-role. It's difficult speak without prejudice and negativity. As a wise mother you understand the price a family pays for having an inadequate father. You can compare it to the disaster of a ship-wrecked boat with drowning children, and parents unable to save anyone.

How can you develop the skill of validating and confirming the father of your children?

It's important to <u>simply</u> state what you want to validate and do so with conviction and confidence. "Jim, I admire your ability to make us all laugh. The kids love it when you do your clown thing. It relieves us all of the seriousness of what we are going through. Thank you." "Honey, the kids love it when you get down and play with them. They obey so much more readily after one of your play sessions. Thank you."

Clearly and persuasively speak of what you have seen and would like to encourage. "Jim, I noticed that you were reading to Julie today. I thought it was so sweet the way you let her try to figure out the words. I know she loved it. She waits for you to come home. She is so excited about reading for you. Thank you." "Honey, remember the time you and Jimmy worked in the garden? He still talks about it. He wants to go with you and buy more seeds. He is hoping you will ask him to go this Saturday. Thanks for being such a great dad."

Affirmation is one of the greatest gifts you can give. Although he loves his child, he may lack confidence in his parenting skills. He does not have the benefit of spending most of his day with his children while they teach him how to be their dad. That is why he must make the most of the precious time when he is actually involved with them. You can help him use that time wisely.

Questions:

1 List three things you can do to affirm your husband in his role as Dad.

_____

_____

_____

_____

2 In what two areas does he most need affirming?

_____

_____

_____

_____

3 Is it easy for you to affirm him in his role as Dad? Explain why or why not.

_____

_____

_____

_____

4 Name two difficulties for you in affirming him.

_____

_____

_____

_____

5 Give one example of how your affirming him has made a difference in his life, your life and your child's life.

_____

_____

_____

_____

Prayer

eavenly Father,
I would like to be able
to affirm my husband
in his role as dad.
Please help me.
Amen

CHAPTER THREE

Course Correction:
Finding True North

hat happens when your husband is not spending time with your child or does not correct the child lovingly? How do you react when you notice obvious slip-ups?

Should you step in and address your husband's way of relating to the child? Yes, you should, because at such times dad needs help to find true north, while you are temporarily captain of the parenting boat. You can broach the subject by saying gently, "Honey, there is another way you could handle this." Your concern is that if his conduct remains unchecked, his relationship with the child will suffer down the road. You cannot afford to wait until he recognizes his mistake.

If you communicate well with your husband, the benefits are huge. Your home will experience profound peace, happiness, and a grateful dad. His facial expression will give evidence that he has had a change of heart due to your intervention.

How can you be certain that it is right to intervene? Here, as everywhere else, you have to rely on God's standards, which he reveals in his Word. The wise wife is a woman of God's Word. You understand that the issue here is what God's Word shows you. First and foremost you let God's Word do its work in you. Before you try to remove the splinter in your husband's eye, you let God remove the beam from your own eye.

Also, you can help your husband more easily if you understand the difference between reproof, correction and instruction.

You *reprove* him with a look or a scowl, and you hope he will catch your look and change accordingly, but this approach usually doesn't work. On the contrary, it can build up resentment because your husband may feel censored by every raised eyebrow or glance when he gets involved with the children.

You *correct* with words. You might say, "This is what I have noticed... Have you noticed that, too?" or "My concern is this... Am I being overly concerned?" "Could this be done differently?" This allows your husband to reflect, communicate and participate in evaluating the problem; any needed change, and to adopt a different approach.

Instruction occurs when you lovingly share some ideas with your husband. You take into account that he, too, may observe certain things you do, which he would want you to change. Be careful not to let this degenerate into a tit-for-tat roller coaster ride where you pick on his dad skills and he picks on your mom skills.

Keep in mind the following principles regarding course correction:

1. Your words are your "rod of correction." What you say and how you say it can either tear him down or build him up.

2. To correct or not to correct is an important consideration. But even more important is when and where to correct — never in front of the children and never at the spur of the moment. Consider carefully what you want to bring up, what you would like to see changed or improved, and how you are willing to help him.

3. Correcting someone you love is not easy; because you are deeply concerned that you might offend him. If you don't really love him, you will not care if he is hurt. Make sure your love shines through your correction.

4. Better to deal with an issue earlier than later. If you wait too long, additional issues may cloud your thinking and emotions, and you may be tempted to "dump" on him.

5. Practice correcting your husband on smaller issues before you attempt to correct his parenting style. You are the only person who really knows his idiosyncrasies. Be mindful of the fact that you have the power to make or break him.

6. Remember "to be kindly affectionate to one another... in honor giving preference to one another". (Rom 12:10)

Practical applications:

1. Look for signs that he will be receptive to what you have to say.

2. Choose a time when neither of you is preoccupied with other things.

3. Start with a simple statement: "Can I tell you what I see happening?"

4. End with: "What can I do to help?"

5. Remember that a little correction goes a long way. Be patient about waiting for his change.

6. Avoid correction discussions during "date night" or immediately when he comes home from work.

7. Bear in mind that his willingness to receive course correction from you is directly proportional to your own openness to receive his advice for you. Do you respond defensively or get hurt? Do you hold a grudge? Can you show genuine gratitude for his input into your parenting style?

There isn't a lot of room for error when you attempt to guide your husband into a course correction. There isn't a lot of grace when it is done wrong. But if you are wise and patient you can learn what works and what doesn't, and the benefits your family reaps are well worth the effort.

Questions:

1 Is it easy for you to receive correction?

_____
_____
_____
_____

2 List two things you feel you would like to correct in your husband's parenting style.

_____
_____
_____
_____

3 Are you kind and loving when you see an area that needs correcting? Or do you get fearful and defensive of your style?

_____
_____
_____
_____

4 When do you find your husband is most receptive to talking about doing something different regarding parenting?

_____
_____
_____
_____

5 Have you learned from correcting at the wrong time, wrong way, etc.?

_____
_____
_____
_____

Prayer

Heavenly Father,
Give me a gentleness
of speech when
correcting
my husband.
Amen

CHAPTER FOUR

Leadership:
Who Is Captain of What Boat?

he issue of who is captain of the family boat may not matter much until the boat is shipwrecked on the sea. Then failure and lack of skills become evident. Then the man and the woman who once upon a time fell in love and promised to cherish each other for the rest of their lives may choose to live on separate islands.

The increasing love between you and your husband led to your becoming Mom and Dad—a family. And now you may discover that what seemed to be a sturdy and sound boat turns out to be nothing more than a flimsy raft, unable to support the burdens and responsibilities of the captain and crew.

Churches often expound on the burdens and responsibilities of being a dad, especially on Father's Day. In this context he is held up as a representative of God in the home. You don't argue with that. You want to believe that the very best qualities in your man will emerge in his role as dad.

What are those qualities?

1. Kindness: relating gently to your son or daughter and consistently reflecting affection and approval.
2. Diligence: demonstrating a steady, earnest, and energetic effort to fulfill all the duties of a dad.
3. Wisdom: knowing and understanding more than he appears to know and understand.

4. Loyalty: faithful to you, and your children regardless of the cost.

5. Strength: able and willing to walk the walk, not merely talk the talk.

6. Humility: has a winsome way with you and your child.

7. Reliability: competent as a man, a lover, faithful husband, provider, dad, and maintainer of house and home.

8. Fitness: uniquely equipped to meet his responsibilities. Willing to learn what he does not know, and able to follow through.

9. Expertise: a captain who is chosen because of his qualifications. When it comes to captains, the crew does not appoint the captain except in the case of mutiny. Captains are not the popular choice of the people on the boat. He is appointed before the boat sets sail. After all, the owner of the boat wants it back intact, with all the cargo.

10. Valor: has strength of mind and spirit that enables him to face danger with firmness. He is the cream of the crop.

11. Tried and true: a man with experience who has passed through trials and tests successfully.

12. Bravery: not afraid of the unknown; savoring life's adventure. He takes necessary risks to supply his crew and ship with everything they need.

13. Courage: he can endure opposition and obstacles and steer the boat competently.

14. Cheerful servant: can you imagine a captain who is not willing to serve the best interests of his crew? Such a man would not deserve to be captain. Humor aids every storm.

15. Skilled warrior: able to defend his crew and cargo, encourages everyone on the boat and brings out the best in them.

Over the last twenty years I have noticed a troubling phenomenon: Dads seem to be asleep in their boats. The course of the boat is uncharted. The destination is unsure. The crew is scattered. The captain has abandoned the helm.

Many boats are in practicality without a captain, and they sink. The survivors are adrift in flimsy rubber crafts, subject to storms, predators, and the elements. In retrospect, after the shipwreck and while fighting for life, suddenly it becomes clear how many mistakes were made. Yet how many small course adjustments could have kept this disaster from happening?

When a boat on the sea of parenting goes down in divorce, no one remains unscathed. The loss not only affects the crew, but other boats, crews and captains who will set sail in the future.

Does it sound simplistic to you that the Captain of our salvation, Jesus Christ, has a specific plan for every parenting boat? He has appointed the husband to be the captain of his family. Why? Because He wants the boat and its crew and cargo to reach the designated port safely. The human captain is not perfect, but must allow Jesus Christ to develop him. Jesus knew that a boat could not do well with two captains. One captain is appointed while the boat is still on shore. The crew doesn't wait to choose a captain while at sea. Jesus holds one man responsible for the boat, the crew and the crossing. One man can be trained. One man can be directed as long as he is willing to take on the challenge, even though he is not yet a veteran captain.

You understand the importance of the captain, his responsibilities and the hardships of that position. You, his wife, are his anchor in the storm, his compass in the night, and the wind in his sails. He can never get to shore without you. He needs to discern that parenting plan from his Captain – Jesus. He, your husband is captain of the boat. He is responsible for each of the crew members.

Questions:

1 Is it easy or difficult for you to help your husband be captain of the boat? (Yes/No) Explain.

_____

_____

_____

_____

2 Is he willing to be captain? (Yes/No) How do you know?

_____

_____

_____

_____

3 What two things would you like to see changed?

_____

_____

_____

_____

4 Is reconciliation easy or difficult after his mistakes as captain? Give an example.

_____

_____

_____

_____

5 Do you and does he recognize how important your role is as he leads?

_____

_____

_____

_____

Prayer

eavenly Father,
I believe that your
gift to me and our family
is my husband, the
captain of our boat.
Help me daily
to believe this
more and more.
Amen

CHAPTER FIVE

Correction, Discipline and Training:
Charting the Course

hildren definitely change a marriage. When a man and a woman fall in love, they marry and adjust to each other as husband and wife. This is easier for some than for others. Growing up in a large family can either help or hinder the marital relationship bond.

What once was considered a normal upbringing appears today like a sheltered life. In our society many young people experience a number of traumas on the way to marriage, such as drug dependency, abuse, divorce, premarital sex, teen pregnancy, or gang membership. Music, TV, movies and the internet portray as normal what used to be considered wrong, immoral or deviant.

Marriage is often viewed as a temporary live-in situation. News and entertainment shows are filled with break-ups and bitter divorce suits. Long marriages are more exceptional today than twenty or thirty years ago.

Today's newlyweds, who have passed through a gauntlet of negative experiences in their childhood, must first discard this baggage in order to build a sound and healthy life together. When they succeed a whole new world awaits them.

When this new mother and father are launched into a life-long adventure as parents they must work out a plan or method of bringing their child to maturity, charting a life course for him or her. Wouldn't it be interesting to interview new parents about the goals they have for their children? Would that include drugs at thirteen? How would dad feel about a promiscuous daughter? How many children could their daughter have or their son father before graduating from high school? Would so-called "alternative lifestyles" be a part of their parental plans?

If these parents could "word out" a positive outcome to their parenting, what would they insist on integrating into the life of their child? Good citizenship? Knowing God? A sense of security and peace with himself or herself?

Mom and dad may discover along the way that they have different values, different ideas of what is right or wrong, and different standards for their child's behavior. Such differences can be divisive. At that point, divorce may appear as an easy out. Even though the kids are told to work out their relationships within the family, moms and dads think they have a "right" to separate. But the kids don't need to be torn from their home, their rooms, friends, neighborhood or extended family on either side of the family. Hopefully each child has been corrected and disciplined to promote unity and harmony in the home. Now Mom and Dad should take a dose of their own medicine and work out their differences.

A man on a weekend boating trip can easily lose track of time while he is in a world far away from his daily grind. Likewise, a man raising his children can lose himself in other activities, often away from his children, while time races by and his children grow up. Dad can be so involved in his work that he is surprised when his children leave home and start their own families. Where has he been while they were growing up?

Raising a child consists of correction, discipline and training. The wise mother understands that her husband must be involved in all three. As mother you must correct the child's attitude on a daily basis. Occasionally you need to discipline your child away from undesirable conduct and attitudes. You train your child by taking the initiative in your relationship with him or her, thereby opening new doors and walking through each door together—mom, dad and child.

You need the threefold cord of correction, discipline and training when you chart the life course for your child. What holds this cord together is communication — regularly discussing the pros, the cons, and the possibilities. Yes, dreaming is also part of parenting. It is sad to see a child not yet eighteen thrown overboard as if he or she were an adult. Left to himself and his own devices, the child is snatched up by the storms, waves and hidden hazards of the sea. The parents may try to save him, but it is too late. They failed to chart the child's course. He was allowed to chart his own course across the sea and to fall overboard. The immediate purpose of the sailing then changes from enjoyment to salvage.

Charting their child's course requires agreement and unity between mom and dad.

A wise Mom recognizes how important this is and invests time and energy helping Dad get involved in the issues along the way. Dad may be busy. He may be disinterested. But you love your man and you can find a way to his heart. You can mobilize him and spark his interest in the path your child is taking.

Life seems easier without children — just the two of you focusing on each other. It requires no discussion of who will pick up the kids, who will take them to sports practice, and who will discipline them. So often it is the harder things that are the most rewarding — so it is with raising children. As parents you must intentionally chart the course of your family.

Questions:

1 Which of you finds correction, discipline and/or training easiest?

_____

_____

_____

_____

2 Name three of the most difficult aspects of discipline.

_____

_____

_____

_____

3 Has it been easy/difficult for you and your husband to "get on the same page" regarding correction, discipline and training? Give an example.

_____

_____

_____

_____

4 How have you involved and allowed your child to be part of this process?

_____

_____

_____

_____

5 Name two things you would like to see changed in you and in your husband regarding this area.

_____

_____

_____

_____

Prayer

*H*eavenly Father,
I would like a miracle
— give my husband and
me agreement in the
discipline and correction
of our children.
Amen

CHAPTER SIX

God's Idea of a Dad:
He Clothes His Children

od created Adam and Eve and established them upon the earth. And He gave them children. From the beginning, God conferred equal value on both mother and father.

Today's popular culture holds dads in contempt regarding the proper role they ought to play in their children's lives and the family as a whole. No wonder fathers have come to believe the lie that they have little or no value. Many are convinced that anyone can fill their place while their wives, who used to be their best friends and lovers, kick them out of the home, and the courts routinely separate them from their children.

A lot of divorces are not due to abuse or mistreatment or the man's failure to provide, care for or love his family. In many cases, disregard for God has destroyed the family covenant agreement. By and large, the American family is no longer guided by the standards of the Bible. Even among church-goers the divorce rate is said to be no different than in the secular world. Many times we relish what is dear to us only when we no longer have it. What a blessing it is, therefore, when parents decide right from the start that they will not consider divorce. They commit to work out their problems; not for the children's sake, but for God's sake. Once the thread that holds everyone together is broken, shattered lives will bob on the sea of parenting and many never recover from the experience.

God has made it clear how highly He values the father of the family. The god-fearing wife will attach the same significance to her husband's role in the lives of their children as God does. What value, exactly, does God place on the father?

What is God's idea of a dad?

The last two verses of the Old Testament tell us that God "...will send Elijah the prophet before the coming of the great and dreadful day of the Lord: And he shall turn the heart of the fathers to the children, and the heart of the children to their fathers..." (Mal 4:5-6 kjv). In God's mind, fathers play an integral part in the lives of their children.

In three biblical accounts, an interesting phenomenon takes place between father and child.

1. When God expelled Adam and Eve from the garden (Gen. 3:21) we are told: "Unto Adam also and to his wife did the Lord God make coats of skins, and he clothed them."

2. In Genesis 37:3, "Now Israel loved Joseph more than all his children because he was the son of his old age: and he made him a coat of many colors."

3. Luke 15:22 says, "But the father said to his servants, bring forth the best robe, and put it on him..." Matt. 6:30 ties it all together: "Wherefore, if God so clothe the grass of the field, which today is, and tomorrow is cast into the oven, shall he not much more clothe you...?"

Adam and Eve sinned less, Joseph went through hard times more easily, and the prodigal son recovered from hard times more quickly, all because a father clothed them. Herein lies the essential value of a father. He is present in his children's lives. He <u>clothes</u> them. This clothing is a spiritual covering with real life benefits.

Children who have a loving, caring father in their lives are the better for it. Various studies report this:

1. Children with fathers in the home are less likely to repeat a grade in school, less likely to drop out of school, and more likely to excel. These children enjoy school and engage in extracurricular activities. They are less likely to become delinquents. Adolescent girls are significantly less likely to be sexually active.

2. Children from fatherless homes are more likely to commit suicide as teenagers and make up a higher percentage of runaways and homeless children. Eighty percent of rapists come from fatherless homes. Eighty-five percent of all youths in prison come from fatherless homes. Daughters without a father are 53% more likely to marry as teenagers. If a teen lives without a father he or she is nine times more likely to become a high school dropout.

Most dads are eager for a little recognition. They do their job; they work hard, and take care of the cars, home repairs and many other tasks on the "honey-do list." When it comes to affirming him as a dad, no one is better qualified than you, his wife and the mother of his children, to give the best or worst testimony. Filled with God's wisdom, you are the one that can transform him into the greatest dad ever.

You guide him through the maze of his role. With love and tenderness you help him see the dangers, hidden sand bars and quick currents as you sail the sea of parenting together. You do this because you love him and want to see him succeed.

As soon as you lose your love and admiration for him, you will stop building him up as a dad. When you stop thinking about him and start thinking mainly about yourself, you are on the road to unhappiness and in many cases, divorce.

"Thank you," "Would you, please," or "When you have time" are phrases that are sometimes forgotten shortly after leaving the port with your new baby. These are not mere words, however; they do a number on the heart of the captain. Additional phrases that continue to build dad are: "Honey, I love to watch you with the kids!" "They love it when you take the time to be/play with them."

Your husband is not actually asking for this type of acknowledgement, but it makes a world of difference when you are generous with your admiration of him as a dad. When couples divorce, is it because they hate their children? Is it because they want nothing to do with them any more? Not at all; but they have learned to hate each other as husband and wife. Long ago, their love burned like a flame, but its embers are dying. Now dead! They may continue to dislike each other throughout the shared custody of their children.

Is this what you, the virtuous wife, would want? If you could make a difference wouldn't you give it a try? Sometimes it just takes a little to make a huge difference. If you honestly believe that your husband has value as a dad and you are proactive in building him up in his role, then you enable him to believe in himself, and he will act like the dad you believe he can be.

Questions:

1 How did your mother treat your Dad? How did this influence how you saw your Dad?

_____
_____
_____
_____

2 Describe your Dad and how you saw him in your life when you were under eighteen years of age.

_____
_____
_____
_____

3 Has your opinion/view of your Dad changed now that you have children? (Yes/No) Explain.

_____
_____
_____
_____

4 Describe your husband as family leader — his strengths, his weaknesses.

_____
_____
_____
_____

5 Give three examples of how you have been able to help him become a better Dad. How do your children see their Dad?

_____
_____
_____
_____

Prayer

*H*eavenly Father,
I would like to see my
husband as you see him.
Open my eyes
to see.
Amen

CHAPTER SEVEN

A Dad's Ministry:
Giving Life

s a prudent wife, you determine not only the value of a dad in the home, you also understand the ministry of a dad in the life of his children. Let's examine two questions: What constitutes a ministry, and how is being a dad a ministry?

WHAT CONSTITUTES A MINISTRY?

Seven criteria comprise a ministry.

1. *Ordained by God*

   Adam was the first dad. No other man fathered a child before Adam. And when God created the first man, he also endowed him with the capacity, the ability, the necessary skills and talents to be a dad.

2. *A gift from God to those that are being served*

   In creating Adam, God was giving a gift to Adam's offspring. His first child established Adam as a dad. All of Adam's fatherhood ultimately drew upon the skills and talents God placed within him to help his child grow into a mature adult.

3. *God's representative on earth*

   Every Father's Day preachers throughout the Christian world challenge earthly fathers to follow the example of their Heavenly Father, because God has established Himself as the supreme model of fatherhood.

4. *Fulfilling a specific role or purpose*

   A man can do many things here on earth. He can be many things to many people, but when he becomes a dad he takes on a very specific role and purpose. He is expected to be a provider for his children and care for them. He is expected to preserve that life, train his children, and release them into adult life.

5. *Accountable to God for the results*

   A dad participates in the creation of life, but he is not the originator of that life. He needs to give an account for that life to its Originator. I believe all dads will have to answer the question "What did you do with the lives I entrusted to your care?"

6. *Initiated by God*

   Adam, the first man, didn't come to God seeking life. God decided "to make man." God, having made man, also made woman. And God created man and woman with the ability and mandate to reproduce. Adam's offspring made him a dad.

7. *Divine pattern*

   At one point, God began to refer to a group of people as His Own People. He was their Father, they were His children. There are many examples in the Bible that portray God relating to his children and that gives dads a model for relating to their children.

How Is Being a Dad a Ministry?

Do these seven criteria apply to dads? Absolutely! Are the duties and responsibilities of a dad reflected in these seven criteria? Yes! What, then, is the ministry of a dad in the lives of his children?

A dad who views the relationship with his child as a ministry, most certainly becomes a better Dad because he understands that his presence in the home and his availability to his child is the most important ingredient of his role.

Giving and sustaining life is the hallmark of a dad's ministry to his child. A man becomes a dad as he participates in bestowing life. He sustains and nurtures that life when he relates positively and supportively. How a dad relates to his child either sustains and nurtures life or produces death.

> *The ministry of a dad is to produce and encourage life.*

A Dad is recognized as he does eight specific things:

1. Bestows life through procreation.

2. Has a dream for his child.

3. Models life until he dies.

4. Provides for his child while he is growing up.

5. Understands life because of his own life experiences and maturity.

6. Encourages living a full and meaningful life in service to others.

7. Teaches his child to love life.

8. Releases his child to another journey when the time is right.

Can you show me a wife who would not want her husband to become this kind of dad! What price would you pay to have the man you love with all your heart be like that?

Money won't buy it. As a matter of fact, you pay the price by your willingness to work with him. But how?

1. Rely on faith in God's plan and purpose that every home and family needs a father who is involved in the lives of his children.

2. Stand on the conviction that God established the human family with a mother and a father raising their sons and daughters together. This is God's pattern for the family.

3. Determine to be intentional about your strategy for helping your husband become the best dad he can be.

4. Pray together. Take the initiative and introduce good books to your husband, read them together with him, make time to discuss them, have intimate sharing times about your roles as mother and father.

5. Love him so deeply that you are willing to lay down your life in your continued efforts to nurture him and meet his needs.

6. Take risks by bringing up issues before they are beyond a solution.

7. Never accuse nor excuse.

8. Be tenderhearted and loving to your husband on his journey to being a great dad.

It is almost impossible to estimate the widespread effects a shipwreck on the parenting sea has on a family. There is the loss of unity and love for one another, the loss of identity and ability to serve others. For the rest of their lives, individual family members suffer heartaches that never completely heal. The loss extends to our communities and the world, which lose the healthy contributions this family could have made.

What do you think: Can you afford not to get involved in the making of a great dad? Are you ready to give everything you've got to help your husband on this journey and ensure the health and happiness of your family?

Questions:

1 Give an example of how your Dad encouraged your life.

_____

_____

_____

_____

2 Give two examples of how your Dad failed to model and encourage life.

_____

_____

_____

_____

3 List three examples of how your husband — in his role as Dad — produces and bestows life.

_____

_____

_____

_____

4 List two examples of how your husband teaches about life.

_____

_____

_____

_____

5 List three things you can do to help your husband understand and encourage life.

_____

_____

_____

_____

Prayer

eavenly Father,
Help me to help my
husband give and sustain
life in our home.
Amen

CHAPTER EIGHT

Improving Communication Skills:
When to Paint the Boat

mprovements require hard work. "Painting the boat" refers to your efforts to move your husband to the next level of interpersonal skills. When is it wise for you to attempt this? It is relatively easy to paint the boat right after construction. By comparison this would be courtship and early marriage. You can help your husband develop these two important skills: communication and expressing emotions.

A. Communication

Communication is "a process by which information is exchanged between individuals through a common system of symbols, signs, or behavior."

1. *"A process"*

   Sharing information with your husband is a learning process that lasts a lifetime.

   Your effectiveness depends on the wisdom you employ in the beginning and along the way. You will soon learn that your communication styles are very different.

   He learns in small increments and only when there is no threat of ridicule or put down. As soon as he senses any degree of insult, he turns off any willingness to learn from you. The fact that he communicates differently is very significant because at first he may not readily share his opinions, or perceptions. If you dismiss his viewpoint or do not give him time to explain himself, you make it much harder for him to want to learn how to communicate with you, and ultimately with your children.

2. *"By which information is exchanged"*

Exchanging information becomes a doorway to intimacy. A "cold shoulder" greeting when your husband comes home will usually result in a cool evening. The longer you leave issues unresolved, the more difficult communication becomes. Make it a habit to deal with differences right away, even if they are unrelated to parenting issues.

Poor communication skills account for a dearth of intimacy. Effective communication begins when you listen attentively and really hear what is on your husband's mind and heart.

3. *"Between individuals"*

Ordinarily, a man wants to marry a woman who is his equal. He wants to relate as a loving husband to a loving wife, not as a master to a servant. He wants to give you his best, just as you want to give him your best. Both of you realize that there must be give-and-take in your relationship. Communication improves exponentially as both of you are willing to defer to your partner. If one of you ever loses a sense of personal identity in the course of your marriage, you can be sure that one is dying.

4. *"Through a common system of symbols, signs or behavior"*

This special system starts developing when you date and continues to improve during courtship and early marriage. It finds expression in glances, facial expressions, a smile, a frown, a specific word, or silence. In time all these come to mean more than words alone. It is easy to see the importance of establishing and refining your particular symbols, signs and behaviors early in your relationship.

B. Expressing Emotions

If you are wise, you will help your husband develop this important skill first of all when he communicates with you, and then as he relates to your child. Your husband has emotions, but others may have taught him to not express his emotions openly. He is aware that his choice of words often communicates certain emotions, but leaves out others. He may allow those emotions to surface only when he is alone. Perhaps he rarely gets emotional in positive ways expressing love and tenderness, but has no trouble showing negative feelings like anger and frustration. You can help him with great tenderness to express the positive and control the negative.

Much depends on how you respond to his frustrations. As you respond with understanding, he learns more effective ways to express himself. When you respond lovingly to him, even when he is unable to express affection, you help him learn to respond more quickly with a genuine "I love you!" or "I'm sorry!"

Touch-ups

Touch-ups to your communication, relationship or parenting skills are only minimal and are done while you are secure on deck. They are the light maintenance that builds upon established ways of communicating. A glance or wink can convey to him the message:

"Let's do this differently" or "Let's discuss it later."

Keep in mind that any painting or touch-up needs to take place in private, away from children, other family members or friends. Egos are at stake. Avoid embarrassing him and yourself in front of others. In this way you can prevent the expression of hard feelings or words that would be impossible to take back later.

You will want to become a proficient painter of the boat because then you can guide your husband one step at a time to the place where he will be able to express appropriate feelings readily in word and conduct toward you and your children. Remember that he will immediately spot manipulation that would cause him to resist your efforts. If you don't believe in him, he feels belittled. This communicates to him that you have given up on him.

But if you love him and endeavor to serve him, he can accept your help without losing face. If you botch it up because you lack confidence, or are not willing to defer to your husband, you can lose what you could have gained. What you stand to gain is his respect, love and admiration as he comes to appreciate your love for him in putting up with him in the early years of your marriage. The result? He is eager to let you know that he loves you and that he wants to be a great dad!

Questions:

1 Give an example of how your parents communicated over challenging issues.

_____

_____

_____

_____

2 Give two examples of how your communication skills have improved during the years of your marriage.

_____

_____

_____

_____

3 List one weakness in your exchanging information with your husband.

_____

_____

_____

_____

4 List two ways you and your husband can build better communication skills.

_____

_____

_____

_____

5 How has your ability to talk to one another and to share your points of view <u>improved over the years</u>? Give several examples.

_____

_____

_____

_____

Prayer

eavenly Father,
Give me the grace to
tame my tongue.
Please!
Amen

10727874R00034

Made in the USA
Charleston, SC
29 December 2011